INTRODUC

CU00944916

In my work as a creative business consultant, I hear from my clients again and again that they just don't seem to have enough hours in the day to complete their work. We're all searching for ways to use our time more effectively, to get more things done, and to simplify our task load. In fact, I think a lot of us spend far too much time thinking about how we could spend our time more wisely.

Too often, our minutes, hours, and days just seem to slip by and looking back, it can be hard to see where all that time went. You know you've been working and you feel busy, yet you may not feel as accomplished as you'd like. When we're in the deep trenches of work, it can often be hard to take the necessary steps back to look at the big picture and think about what to do next. What is the task that will actually propel you and your work forward, rather than keep you treading water? How can you control your work instead of simply responding to it?

This notebook is a space for you to keep track of one of your most valuable resources—your time. It's a to-do list, a productivity tracker, and fresh encouragement for thinking about how to best get stuff done. Each page presents a new way for you to consider how you're working and how you can improve. As you fill these pages, you'll begin to notice patterns that emerge about how you spend your time, which will in turn help you see how you can work more efficiently in the future.

Make It Happen! is designed to get your wheels turning and to help you determine what you can accomplish on any given day. Setting goals—big and small—and checking them off a list feels good. It can provide you with real satisfaction, which can reinvigorate how you feel when it comes to your workload. In this journal, you'll find plenty of space for to-do lists and ways to measure your overall productivity, along with time management tips, spots to track when you focus the best, and prompts to help you think about where to most effectively spend your time. Activity charts will also help you *really* see how much time a task takes: for example, if your yoga class is an hour, but it takes a combined two hours to get your gear, get ready, get to the yoga studio, and get home, then you just spent three hours on yoga. Getting your routine tasks done tends to take more time than you think . . .

This notebook will also challenge you to think about what you could do differently in your day or how to envision a task differently. Maybe you could swap some of the time you spend reading blogs with cleaning up your feed reader so you waste less time tomorrow on sites you don't enjoy. Maybe to finally complete that long-avoided task you need to list out what it would actually take to finish it. Do you need approval from an outside source, to connect people or projects to finish something up, or is it an even simpler solution you simply hadn't considered?

Managing your time well isn't all about detailed lists and check boxes and moving as quickly as possible from one task to the next. It's really about noticing the details of your day and how you handle them. This notebook challenges you to thoughtfully consider your everyday tasks in order to work smarter and to redefine your work on a daily basis. If you have half an hour, what can you do? What things on your daily to-do list use five minutes or less? If one of your overall goals is to finally organize your overflowing inbox, set aside ten minutes to do just that. Or make a deal with yourself: each time you hit the refresh button to check for new email, delete or file at least five that are just sitting in there. And remember: not all pleasurable time spent is time wasted. Breaks help keep your mind sharp and energized to move on to your next activity. There's a big difference between goofing off and taking intentional breaks to give your mind a rest.

There is no way to use this journal incorrectly. Your time is yours and only you know the best way to use it. I encourage you to envision how you want to feel at the end of your day and spend your time working toward those feelings. It takes practice, but as you grow more efficient, you'll have more time to do all the other things that make you happy. If you find yourself getting off track, remember, you get to start again tomorrow. The only thing that all of us have in common is that we each have the same amount of time to get things done. How are you going to spend your time?

Let's Make It Happen Together,

Kari Chapin

MAKE IT HAPPEN!

- [ ]
- [ ]
- [ ]
- [ ]

NOTES

BREAK IT DOWN

	1 HR	**2** HRs	**3** HRs	**4** HRs	**5** HRs	**6** HRs	**7** HRs	**8** HRs

WORKING

BREAKS

GOOFING OFF

> What task took the most time today?

> How can I improve tomorrow?

MY TIME TODAY

8 AM

9 AM

10 AM

11 AM

12 PM

1 PM

2 PM

3 PM

4 PM

5 PM

6 PM

7 PM

NOTES

I COULD SWAP

	FOR	
	FOR	
	FOR	
	FOR	
	FOR	
	FOR	

NOTES

❯ I can spend _____ minutes on

_____

❯ I spent _____ working on

_____

❯ It takes me _____ to

_____

NOTES

GET IT DONE!

❯ Today:

❯ This week:

❯ This month:

Before you begin, visualize your perfect day or even just the perfect hour. Work toward that.

MAKE IT HAPPEN!

- [ ]
- [ ]
- [ ]
- [ ]

NOTES

BREAK IT DOWN

DATE ___ / ___ / ___

	1 HR	2 HRs	3 HRs	4 HRs	5 HRs	6 HRs	7 HRs	8 HRs
WORKING								
BREAKS								
GOOFING OFF								

❯ What task took the most time today?

_____

_____

_____

❯ How can I improve tomorrow?

_____

_____

_____

_____

MY TIME TODAY

8 AM

9 AM

10 AM

11 AM

12 PM

1 PM

NOTES

2 PM

3 PM

4 PM

5 PM

6 PM

7 PM

NOTES

Segment your to-do list. Write your list
in chunks of time rather than just tasks.

WHAT WOULD IT TAKE TO...

FINISH

?

REACH

?

PLAN

?

IMPLEMENT

?

IN LESS THAN FIVE MINUTES I CAN:

IN LESS THAN ONE HOUR I CAN:

IN A DAY I CAN:

TIME TO REFLECT

WHAT TASKS CAN YOU DELEGATE TODAY?

Do everything on your list that takes
ten minutes or less right now.

MAKE IT HAPPEN!

- [ ]
- [ ]
- [ ]
- [ ]

NOTES

BREAK IT DOWN

DATE   /   /

	1 HR	**2** HRs	**3** HRs	**4** HRs	**5** HRs	**6** HRs	**7** HRs	**8** HRs
WORKING								
BREAKS								
GOOFING OFF								

❯ What task took the most time today?

_____

_____

_____

_____

❯ How can I improve tomorrow?

_____

_____

_____

_____

_____

MY TIME TODAY

8 AM

9 AM

10 AM

11 AM

12 PM

1 PM

NOTES

2 PM

3 PM

4 PM

5 PM

6 PM

7 PM

NOTES

Stuck on a task? Set it aside until later and
let your brain focus elsewhere for a while.

❯ I focus best when:

❯ I'd like more time for:

❯ I see the greatest results when:

❯ I lose steam when:

I COULD SWAP

	FOR	
	FOR	
	FOR	
	FOR	
	FOR	
	FOR	

NOTES

MY TIME MANAGEMENT STRATEGY

❯ I can save time by:

_____

_____

_____

_____

_____

_____

❯ I feel best when I spend my time:

_____

_____

_____

_____

_____

I'D LIKE TO SPEND MY TIME

DOING MORE OF:	DOING LESS OF:

BEFORE LUNCH

BEFORE DINNER

BEFORE I CALL IT A DAY

MAKE IT HAPPEN!

- [ ]
- [ ]
- [ ]
- [ ]

NOTES

BREAK IT DOWN

DATE [/ /]

	1 HR	2 HRs	3 HRs	4 HRs	5 HRs	6 HRs	7 HRs	8 HRs

WORKING

BREAKS

GOOFING OFF

> What task took the most time today?

> How can I improve tomorrow?

MY TIME TODAY

8 AM

9 AM

10 AM

11 AM

12 PM

1 PM

NOTES

NOTES

2 PM

3 PM

4 PM

5 PM

6 PM

7 PM

NOTES

TIME TO REFLECT

DATE / /

> **WHAT ARE SOME THINGS YOU CAN SAY NO TO RIGHT NOW?**

Take a stretch break to get your blood flowing.
Moving your body sharpens your focus.

MAKE IT HAPPEN!

- [ ]
- [ ]
- [ ]
- [ ]

NOTES

BREAK IT DOWN

DATE   /   /

	1 HR	2 HRs	3 HRs	4 HRs	5 HRs	6 HRs	7 HRs	8 HRs

WORKING

BREAKS

GOOFING OFF

> What task took the most time today?

_____

_____

_____

> How can I improve tomorrow?

_____

_____

_____

_____

MY TIME TODAY

8 AM

9 AM

10 AM

11 AM

12 PM

1 PM

2 PM

3 PM

4 PM

5 PM

6 PM

7 PM

NOTES

I COULD SWAP

	FOR	
	FOR	
	FOR	
	FOR	
	FOR	
	FOR	

NOTES

IN LESS THAN FIVE MINUTES I CAN:

IN LESS THAN ONE HOUR I CAN:

IN A DAY I CAN:

Turn off your phone. Shut your door.
What distractions can you eliminate to focus better?

TIME TO REFLECT

❯ I focus best when:

❯ I'd like more time for:

❯ I see the greatest results when:

❯ I lose steam when:

BEFORE LUNCH

BEFORE DINNER

BEFORE I CALL IT A DAY

WHAT WOULD IT TAKE TO...

FINISH

?

REACH

?

PLAN

?

IMPLEMENT

?

GET IT DONE!

❯ Today:

❯ This week:

❯ This month:

What time of day do you work best? How can you arrange
your schedule to do your most important work then?

MAKE IT HAPPEN!

- [ ] _____
- [ ] _____
- [ ] _____
- [ ] _____

NOTES

BREAK IT DOWN

DATE   /   /

	1 HR	**2** HRs	**3** HRs	**4** HRs	**5** HRs	**6** HRs	**7** HRs	**8** HRs
WORKING								

BREAKS								

GOOFING OFF								

❯ What task took the most time today?

_____

_____

_____

_____

❯ How can I improve tomorrow?

_____

_____

_____

_____

_____

MY TIME TODAY

8 AM

9 AM

10 AM

11 AM

12 PM

1 PM

2 PM

3 PM

4 PM

5 PM

6 PM

7 PM

NOTES

> I can spend _____ minutes on

_____

_____

> I spent _____ working on

_____

_____

> It takes me _____ to

_____

_____

TIME TO REFLECT

CHALLENGE YOURSELF TO ONLY CHECK
YOUR EMAIL FIVE TIMES TODAY.

Grant yourself permission to spend time doing something fun. Mental breaks make for better focusing.

MAKE IT HAPPEN!

- [ ] _____
- [ ] _____
- [ ] _____
- [ ] _____
  _____
  _____
  _____
  _____
  _____

NOTES

BREAK IT DOWN

DATE   /   /

	1 HR	2 HRs	3 HRs	4 HRs	5 HRs	6 HRs	7 HRs	8 HRs
WORKING								
BREAKS								
GOOFING OFF								

❯ What task took the most time today?

❯ How can I improve tomorrow?

MY TIME TODAY

8 AM

9 AM

10 AM

11 AM

12 PM

1 PM

NOTES

2 PM

3 PM

4 PM

5 PM

6 PM

7 PM

NOTES

TIME TO REFLECT

KEEP YOURSELF HYDRATED. HOW
MUCH WATER DID YOU DRINK TODAY?

Begin conversations and meetings with phrases like, "I'd like to discuss this for 15 minutes . . ." or "I have 20 minutes to spend on this . . ." Create boundaries with other people around your time.

IN LESS THAN FIVE MINUTES I CAN:

IN LESS THAN ONE HOUR I CAN:

IN A DAY I CAN:

WHAT WOULD IT TAKE TO...

DATE / /

FINISH

?

REACH

?

PLAN

?

IMPLEMENT

?

MAKE IT HAPPEN!

- [ ]
- [ ]
- [ ]
- [ ]

NOTES

BREAK IT DOWN

	1 HR	2 HRs	3 HRs	4 HRs	5 HRs	6 HRs	7 HRs	8 HRs

WORKING

BREAKS

GOOFING OFF

❯ What task took the most time today?

❯ How can I improve tomorrow?

MY TIME TODAY

8 AM

9 AM

10 AM

11 AM

12 PM

1 PM

2 PM

3 PM

4 PM

5 PM

6 PM

7 PM

NOTES

GET IT DONE!

❯ Today:

_____

_____

_____

_____

_____

_____

❯ This week:

_____

_____

_____

_____

_____

_____

❯ This month:

_____

_____

_____

_____

_____

_____

MY TIME MANAGEMENT
STRATEGY

❯ I can save time by:

❯ I feel best when I spend my time:

I'D LIKE TO SPEND MY TIME

DOING MORE OF:	DOING LESS OF:

TIME TO REFLECT

WHAT MOTIVATES YOU? ARE YOU
DEVOTING TIME TOWARD THAT THING?

Do you repeatedly avoid a task? Ask yourself
why and figure out how to offload it.

MAKE IT HAPPEN!

- [ ]
- [ ]
- [ ]
- [ ]

NOTES

BREAK IT DOWN

DATE   /   /

	1 HR	2 HRs	3 HRs	4 HRs	5 HRs	6 HRs	7 HRs	8 HRs
WORKING								
BREAKS								
GOOFING OFF								

> What task took the most time today?

_____

_____

_____

> How can I improve tomorrow?

_____

_____

_____

_____

MY TIME TODAY

8 AM

9 AM

10 AM

11 AM

12 PM

1 PM

2 PM

3 PM

4 PM

5 PM

6 PM

7 PM

NOTES

TIME TO REFLECT

WHAT DID YOU FEEL BEST ABOUT TODAY? DO THAT AGAIN.

Commit to *not* multitasking. Focus on
one thing at a time and then move on.

MAKE IT HAPPEN!

- [ ]
- [ ]
- [ ]
- [ ]

NOTES

BREAK IT DOWN

	1 HR	2 HRs	3 HRs	4 HRs	5 HRs	6 HRs	7 HRs	8 HRs

WORKING

BREAKS

GOOFING OFF

> What task took the most time today?

> How can I improve tomorrow?

MY TIME TODAY

8 AM

9 AM

10 AM

11 AM

12 PM

1 PM

NOTES

2 PM

3 PM

4 PM

5 PM

6 PM

7 PM

NOTES

I COULD SWAP

	FOR	
	FOR	
	FOR	
	FOR	
	FOR	
	FOR	

NOTES

> I can spend _____ minutes on

> I spent _____ working on

> It takes me _____ to

NOTES

GET IT DONE!

❯ Today:

❯ This week:

❯ This month:

Notice what items on your to-do list appear again and again.
How can you simplify this repeat workload?

MAKE IT HAPPEN!

- [ ] _____
- [ ] _____
- [ ] _____
- [ ] _____

_____

_____

_____

_____

_____

NOTES

BREAK IT DOWN

DATE / /

	1 HR	2 HRs	3 HRs	4 HRs	5 HRs	6 HRs	7 HRs	8 HRs
WORKING								
BREAKS								
GOOFING OFF								

❯ What task took the most time today?

_____

_____

_____

❯ How can I improve tomorrow?

_____

_____

_____

_____

_____

MY TIME TODAY

8 AM

9 AM

10 AM

11 AM

12 PM

1 PM

NOTES

DATE   /   /

2 PM

3 PM

4 PM

5 PM

6 PM

7 PM

NOTES

Time three random daily activities today.
How long did it take you to do them?

WHAT WOULD IT TAKE TO...

FINISH

?

REACH

?

PLAN

?

IMPLEMENT

?

IN LESS THAN FIVE MINUTES I CAN:

IN LESS THAN ONE HOUR I CAN:

IN A DAY I CAN:

TIME TO REFLECT

WHAT MAKES YOUR EYES GLAZE OVER?
HOW CAN YOU BETTER APPROACH THAT TASK?

DATE   /   /

Download an app that blocks Internet access for a period of time. See how much more you can get done.

MAKE IT HAPPEN!

- [ ]
- [ ]
- [ ]
- [ ]

NOTES

BREAK IT DOWN

DATE / /

	1 HR	**2** HRs	**3** HRs	**4** HRs	**5** HRs	**6** HRs	**7** HRs	**8** HRs
WORKING								
BREAKS								
GOOFING OFF								

❯ What task took the most time today?

❯ How can I improve tomorrow?

MY TIME TODAY

8 AM

9 AM

10 AM

11 AM

12 PM

1 PM

2 PM

3 PM

4 PM

5 PM

6 PM

7 PM

NOTES